Building
Self-esteem
through
Animal Stories

Animal Storybook No. 2

By Cathy Chargualaf

Animal Storybook No. 2

By Cathy Chargualaf

This belongs to:

Name:________________________

Designed and produced by Cathy Chargualaf

Animal Storybook No. 2: Building Self-Esteem through Animal Stories

Photograph by Steve Torres, Strike A Pose Photography

Balboa Press books may be ordered through booksellers or by contacting:

Balboa Press
A Division of Hay House
1663 Liberty Drive
Bloomington, IN 47403
www.balboapress.com
844-682-1282

ISBN: 978-1-4525-7583-4 (sc)
ISBN: 978-1-4525-7584-1 (e)

Library of Congress Control Number: 2013911655

Print information available on the last page.

Balboa Press rev. date: 04/23/2022

Dedicated to

*My grandchildren Isaiah, Aliyah, Mariah, Abbey, Zoey,
and Briella who fill my heart with joy.*

A special thanks to

*My husband Tom, without him you would not have this book in your
hands, he is my friend, supporter, and the love of my life,*

*My daughter Jasmine, my heart, whom I love so very much,
for being a light in this life,*

My parents for teaching me values that launch my desire to write this book,

*My talented brother Mike, professional illustrator, for providing
positive feedback on my story and illustrations,*

*My Aunt Carol for inspiring me to find the resources
to make this book possible,*

*My friends Joanne, Brenda, Cynthia and Patricia for encouraging
me to write and publish my work; Brandon for scanning my original
art work; Tom and Caroline for supporting and helping me proof my
work; Karl and David for being there to inspire my creativity.*

TABLE OF CONTENTS

Introduction for Parents xi

The Little Giraffe Who Cared 1

The Little Porcupine That Always Helped Others 7

The Little Swan That Knew She Could Do Anything 11

INTRODUCTION FOR PARENTS

Please read first

Thank you for caring enough to give a child a gift that he or she will carry for the rest of their life.

We would love to hear from you how the Animal Storybook and affirmations changed or enhanced your child's self-esteem and self-worth.

Please send all testimonials to:
cathy.chargualaf@ca.rr.com

Instructions:

Sit down with your child. Give yourself enough time to follow through with each story, allowing time for your child's questions. Read each story. The order does not matter. If your child has a favorite animal start with that one first.

After reading a story, ask your child to recall when they helped someone. Have them remember a specific day and time. This will help your child remember what it felt like to help someone. Once your child has the event in mind, ask them to recall what was said, what was done, and how it felt. After your child has told his or her story, let them know how proud you are of them. Then have them recite, as an example, the same affirmation as the little cat, "I am caring."

Supporting your child in his or her own positive affirmation will build self-worth. Remember that praise builds good character and criticism cuts at the very heart of their self-esteem.

THE LITTLE GIRAFFE WHO CARED

Their once was a little giraffe that lived in the jungle. One day, the little giraffe went for a walk. He came to a river and found a little hippo sitting in the water, crying. The little giraffe said, "Hi, are you ok?"

The little hippo turned around, wiped his eyes, and said, "I hurt my toe on a rock in the river. It really hurts." "May I look at your toe?", asked the little giraffe.

The little giraffe sat down next to the little hippo to look at his toe. "You're going to be OK", said the little giraffe.

Just as the little hippo wiped the tears from his eyes, the little giraffe jumped up and said, “I see why your toe is hurting so much. You have a tiny rock under your toenail. May I remove it?”, asked the giraffe. The little hippo said, “Yes, please”.

The little giraffe put his arm around the little hippo and said, “You’re going to be OK”. I will stay here with you until you feel better. OK?”.

The little giraffe stayed with the little hippo until he was feeling better. Later, the little giraffe and hippo said goodbye and went home.

The little giraffe told his mother all about his day. "Do you know what you did today?", said the mother giraffe, "you showed someone that you cared. This is very good, and I am proud of you". "Thanks mom, but it wasn't a big deal.", said the little giraffe.

"Son, you did a wonderful thing, and I am sure you made that little hippo feel better. I want you to know you are a caring person, and now I want you to say, "I am a caring person."".

The little giraffe said, "I am a caring person.", with a big smile on his face.

THE LITTLE PORCUPINE THAT ALWAYS HELPED OTHERS

Their once was a little porcupine that lived in the forest. One day, the little porcupine was outside playing. Suddenly, he heard a small voice saying, "Excuse me, can you help me. I am lost."

"You're lost?" said the little porcupine. "Yes!" said the small mouse, "I just wanted to see what was on the other side of this tree".

"Somehow I got lost and I can't find my home in the rocks". The porcupine looked up and all around, and said, "I know what rocks you're talking about".

"Follow me. You will be OK," said the little porcupine. The small mouse said, "I am so scared. I really miss my mom, dad, brother, and sister."

They passed a tree, went over a green hill, and they walked and walked, until they came to some rocks.

"OK, I think this is it. You are home safe and sound.", said the little porcupine. The family was so happy to see the little mouse.

Later that night the porcupine's mom said, "Sometimes we know things that can help others. This is good when we share it with others. Look how you helped that small mouse find his way home. I am so proud you."

"I want you to know that what you did was a very nice thing and I am sure you made that small mouse feel safe and stopped his family from worrying. I want you to know that you are a helpful person, and now I want you to say, "I am a helpful person".

The little porcupine said, "I am a helpful person" with a big smile on his face.

THE LITTLE SWAN THAT KNEW SHE COULD DO ANYTHING

Their once was a little swan that lived on a pond. One day, the little swan was swimming around the edge of the pond. She wanted to slide across the water, like the other swans. She would practice and practice all day.

"I know I can do this!", said the little swan. She really wanted to glide slowly and smoothly.

"Hi little swan. Do you want to glide on the water? Would you like some help?", said a little fish.

"I want to glide like a beautiful swan. You know, like all the other swans!", said the little swan. The fish remembered that not all swans glide the same. The fish said, "I know you want to be like all the others, but everyone has a different way of being themselves. I will help you find your way.

Close your eyes and think of gliding. Think about how it would feel to glide over the water. Now see yourself gliding. Do you see yourself?". "Yes, wow! It looks so easy.", said the little swan.

"Ok, glide!", said the fish.

"Wow, you are gliding so cool. You make it look so easy to do. Give me five!", said the fish.

That day, the little swan glided home with the biggest smile on her face. She told her mom and dad what happened. Her mom and dad said, "I want you to know that you can do anything you put your mind to. All you have to do is see yourself doing it, and you will do it".

"You can do anything my little swan, and I am so proud of you. Now I want you to say, "I can do anything."".

The little swan said, "I can do anything and that makes me happy.", with a big smile on her face.

About the Author

Cathy Chargualaf is an author and founder of the Life Esteem Wellness Center. She provides positive impact coaching, seminars, and Life Esteem retreats.

Cathy teaches how to use powerful and effective tools to walk consciously and confidently through life's challenges from a centered and balanced place of possibility, opportunity, inner peace, abundance and joy. She helps adults and children increase their self-esteem and self-worth.

She offers a variety of services focused on bringing about physical and emotional well-being. Cathy and her husband, practice in Southern California. Website: www.cathychargualaf.com

Animal Storybooks:

Animal Storybook No. 1

Publisher: Balboa Press

By Cathy Chargualaf

Animal Storybook No. 2

Publisher: Balboa Press

By Cathy Chargualaf

Printed in the United States
by Baker & Taylor Publisher Services